Praise for *Awaken Your Inner Golfer*

"Jerry Brown has cracked the code and unlocked the mysteries of self-discovery by tapping in to the powers of awakening instinct, mindfulness, and meditative practice. Jerry empowers you to become your own golf coach by leading you through a simple process of discovering your natural and instinctive golf swing. This may prove to be the next revolution for twenty-first-century golf. So relax your way into a neuromuscular software update and enjoy a newfound ease, joy, and grace in your golf game and life!"

—KENNETH DIEHL, MPT, GCFP
PHYSICAL THERAPIST, FELDENKRAIS PRACTITIONER

"Jerry Brown's book brings a breath of fresh air to the golf world. Research shows that when we 'play' (rather than 'work at') a sport, our brains and bodies are fully present and our game becomes effortless and optimized. Jerry gives us that permission to truly 'play' golf, and the tools to relax, enjoy, and find our own flow. A must read for every golfer and anyone interested in optimizing their joy in life."

—CARLA HANNAFORD, PhD
BIOLOGIST, AUTHOR, AND
INTERNATIONAL EDUCATIONAL CONSULTANT

"This book offers one of the finest explanations of the power of the subconscious mind. The author is speaking of 'instinctive kinesthetic intelligence'—critical information to incorporate for personal success. Fellow golfers who apply this natural method of self-improvement will experience tremendous results."

—CINDY SKIDMORE
ʼSYCHOLOGICAL KINESIOLOGIST

D0888333

"Here's an excellent example of what is needed in golf instruction today—a book based on the deeper principles of how a fluid golf swing is produced. Bravo to Jerry Brown for a wonderful book that can help golfers improve and enjoy their game."

—STEVEN YELLIN
PRESIDENT OF FLUIDMOTIONGOLF.COM AND
AUTHOR OF *THE 7 SECRETS OF WORLD CLASS ATHLETES*

"In *Awaken Your Inner Golfer*, Jerry Brown returns a missing piece to golf: the fact that it's a game! Through Jerry's playful approach to practice, you can tap in to your kinesthetic intelligence, which innately knows how to move your body. Exhale, smile, give it a go—and play your way to a more enjoyable game!"

—KATHY BROWN, MEd, EDUCATIONAL KINESIOLOGIST
AND AUTHOR OF *EDUCATE YOUR BRAIN*

"The self-learning approach, especially the brain's connection to the process of self-learning and development, should be taken into consideration by all instructors and students of golf."

—MICHAEL HEBRON
PGA HALL OF FAME MEMBER, GOLF INSTRUCTION CONSULTANT,
AND AUTHOR OF *SEE AND FEEL THE INSIDE MOVE THE OUTSIDE*

Awaken Your Inner Golfer

Watch your golf game
Improve and grow
As you awaken
What you already know.

Awaken your
INNER GOLFER

Finding Your Flow

JERRY BROWN

Foreword by Richard William Skurla, DO, CSPOMM

Keep It Simple Golf
SANTA FE, NEW MEXICO

Published by
KEEP IT SIMPLE GOLF MEDIA
PO Box 32632
Santa Fe, NM 87594
www.keepitsimplegolf.com

Editor: Ellen Kleiner

Consultant: Daniel Gibson

Illustrator: Paul Hillman

Cover and interior design and production: Angela Werneke, River Light Media

Author photos: Kitty Leaken

Cover image digital enhancement: Teri Yarbrow

First Edition

This book is designed to provide information and motivation to readers. Its content is the sole expression and opinion of the author, with no warranties or guarantees expressed or implied. Neither the publisher nor the author shall be liable for any physical, psychological, emotional, financial, or commercial damages, including, but not limited to, special, incidental, consequential, or other casualties. Readers are responsible for their own choices, actions, and results.

Printed in Canada

PUBLISHER'S CATALOGING-IN-PUBLICATION DATA

Names: Brown, Jerry (Gerard F.), 1954- author. | Skurla, Richard William, writer of
    foreword.

Title: Awaken your inner golfer : finding your flow / Jerry Brown ; foreword by Richard
    William Skurla.

Description: First edition. | Santa Fe, New Mexico : Keep It Simple Golf Media, [2018]

Identifiers: ISBN: 978-0-9987719-0-8 (wire-bound) | 978-0-9987719-1-5 (eBook) |
    LCCN: 2017903212

Subjects: LCSH: Golf—Training. | Grip (Golf)—Training. | Golf—Physiological aspects. |
    Golf—Psychological aspects. | Muscular sense. | Biomechanics. | Movement,
    Psychology of. | Body-mind centering. | Mind and body. | BISAC: SPORTS &
    RECREATION / Golf.

Classification: LCC: GV979.T68 B76 2018 | DDC: 796.352/3--dc23

1 3 5 7 9 10 8 6 4 2

To ravens, blue jays, and butterflies...
Richard, Rita, and Patty

Acknowledgments

I would like to acknowledge and thank associates and friends who have helped make the content, quality, organization, and design of this book possible, including Ellen Kleiner of Blessingway Authors' Services, Daniel Gibson, Paul Hillman, Angela Werneke, Kitty Leaken, Teri Yarbrow, Dr. Linda Lancaster, John Sherdon, Kate Ciannella, Raymond Young, and Patrick Brockwell.

Contents

Foreword

I was a natural "lefty" athlete. I had played collegiate basket-ball, legion baseball. I inherited most or all of my talent from my dad, who was a three-letter all-star high school state champion. Nevertheless, an effective golf swing eluded me. Whether from the left or right side, mine was never consis-tent, rarely satisfying, and felt like it wasn't me. But I liked the sport. So I decided that perhaps later in life I would take up golf again for the sheer joy of it.

That day arrived when a slender fellow named Jerry came into my clinic and told me he was writing a book about "ex-ploring instinct" in the golf swing. As we became acquainted, I grew intrigued about his book. I knew Jerry's history and noted that he had taken up golf at age ten as a natural, falling in love with the sport. But two years later he had developed double vision as a result of a mass blocking a ventricle in his brain, and he had undergone brain surgery and radiation. Then before his nineteenth birthday he had secondary damage to his auditory nerve and two more surgeries to attempt correc-tion of his double vision. He had also developed a significant secondary spinal scoliosis as a result of the connective tissue distortions that ensued after his brain surgery. Yet despite all these obstacles, by the age of twenty-two he had played collegiate golf and begun consistently winning club champi-onships; he later competed for the Long Island Stoddard Cup

Team. When I questioned him about how he was able to play golf at a competitive level after experiencing such serious physical setbacks, he replied, "At age twelve, after having recovered enough from the brain surgery, I began to relearn the golf swing on my own, in the way a child learns—through feel, instinct, exploration, and discovering what worked for me."

From that statement I inferred quite a bit about how novel his approach to the golf swing might be, as I had been keeping up with the burgeoning field of neuroscience and the brain's ability to restore or make new connections via neuroplasticity. I was quite sure that Jerry could be a prime example of a young brain's miraculous ability to adapt and re-create itself through neuroplasticity. I knew that some of the best examples of such adaptation and re-creation are catalyzed by an individual's adverse experiences, and I wondered if Jerry would be able to relay his discoveries about his new approach to golf.

On the first day I met Jerry at a practice area my question was answered. After observing my swing, checking my grip and stance, he appealed to my instincts and, knowing I used to play baseball, asked me to show him how I would throw the ball sidearm. I did, and he responded, "Make that your only focus, and swing the club with a subtly similar feel." It worked. In a few moments, he had me swinging the pitching wedge as if I had been playing the short game since I was eight years old. Swinging the club this way reminded me of Wes Covington's relaxed batting stance and swing when he had played for the Phillies back in the sixties. It made me laugh and experience joy with every swing.

One day when we were out at a favorite practice area, Jerry

handed me a sand wedge and declared, "Richard, hit a flop shot." I looked at him quizzically and asked, "What is a flop shot?" He replied, "For this, your only focus is to feel the hinge in your wrist on your backswing." Soon I was hitting high, soft flop shots perfectly, one after the other, yet I knew nothing about golf techniques and had little prior training. I was a master of functional biomechanics and osteopathic principles and practice, so I could see how he allowed me to use gravity to leverage the weight of the clubhead, eliminating effort and control and allowing my swing to arise instinctively. But I was still surprised. He smiled at me and commented, "Not many professional golfers can hit that shot as easily as you just did."

Then another day, after a particularly stressful week, we were out playing a round of golf and I could not hit a shot to save my life. I felt like I was struggling with a conflict in my mind and my body was following suit. I had read *Golf in the Kingdom* by Michael Murphy a good while before, but I was at a loss to understand what was off. Then it dawned on me: what if I were subconsciously trying to control something in my life and it was affecting my swing? When I voiced this concern, Jerry's response was, "Let the ball go and walk away from the target right after impact." Sure enough, he had provided the right cue. My next shot on a par 3 landed softly on the green. I grinned. My child genius flooded back into me as I took note of my adult self letting go of control.

Over the years, I have come to realize that most anything we do, whether it is challenging or not and whether we like it or not, can become a road to joyous being when we are fully present with it. Learning to be fully present when playing golf is no exception. If golf is your chosen game, then be a "student of the game," open to gaining greater awareness of its aspects, exploring its potential, and observing how it mirrors life. And if you want some guidance to awaken your instinctive abilities and activate your genius within, this book is well worth taking on your journey.

Richard William Skurla, DO, CSPOMM
AOA Board-Certified Neuromusculoskeletal Medicine

Preface

*It's a miracle that the traditional methods of instruction
have not entirely strangled all learning
and curiosity of inquiry.*

—Albert Einstein

The purpose of *Awaken Your Inner Golfer* is to empower golfers by helping them discover their hidden abilities in the sport; assist them in accessing and developing their instinctive kinesthetic intelligence of the body/mind connection involved in movements; provide tools to encourage them to "be in their bodies" while playing golf rather than "thinking with their minds"; and give them many moments of discovery and joy through a variety of golf exercises. As such, this book concentrates on learning rather than teaching. Expect a deeper understanding of the awesome capacity of your subconscious mind to direct the motor skills needed to hit a golf ball rather than the traditional methods of teaching you to control your golf swing with your conscious mind.

The only instruction in this book involves establishing the foundations of an effective grip and posture since, in my experience, the most common causes of poor golf shots are *a grip and posture that work in opposition to the golfer's natural instincts*. How you place your hands on the golf club and position your torso are critical to establishing a dynamic swing because of their capacity to awaken instinctive abilities. In all my years of golfing, never have I encountered adequate instructions for achieving an effective grip and posture. This book includes simple yet explicit guidelines and illustrations to help build this necessary foundation and, in the final chapter, facilitate the awakening of natural instinctive abilities through a variety of golf exercises.

Awaken Your Inner Golfer is for both beginners and experienced golfers. It is designed to help beginners avoid the frustration of trying to do it right and to help experienced golfers gain new insight.

Exploring the Body/Mind Connection

The content of this book emerged as I was seeking ways to improve my golf game not through conventional methods—engaging the conscious mind to direct muscles of the body to perform certain movements—but from a very different perspective. The catalyst for this exploration was the traumatic event of brain surgery at age twelve. The surgery and radiation that followed left me with a weakened body, compromised hearing, and double vision. Later I sought answers to my medical condition from "experts," resulting in eye surgeries that unfortunately led to more pronounced double vision.

Having started to play golf at age ten, I had come to love the game and the challenges it offered. My physical limitations following surgery obstructed my enjoyment and performance, yet I yearned for the joy and satisfaction inherent in self-improvement. I spent much of my recovery time hitting golf balls with a 9 iron from one end of my family's backyard in a Long Island suburb to the end of my grandmother's backyard next door—an expanse of sixty to seventy yards with a grassy area between thick hedges, a street on one side with occasional vehicular and pedestrian traffic, and a flagpole flanked by thick foliage on the other. I learned to hit the golf ball straight because I did not like looking for golf balls in the foliage or hedges, or the idea of possibly hitting pedestrians or vehicles. The challenge was to trust myself to swing freely and yet land the golf balls in this narrow area. I did not need to be a world-class golfer, just to find my way back to the joy and satisfaction that comes with improvement.

Subsequently, my physical limitations, especially the double vision, prompted me to learn that an effective golf swing is developed not through conscious effort but through tapping in to the body/mind's kinesthetic intelligence. I had to lessen my reliance on visual cues to see exactly how to hit the golf ball and instead *feel* how to make a swing. I had to find ways to depend more on my body's feeling senses and natural adaptive instincts.

My compromised health ultimately led me to the path of holistic wellness. I learned about the body/mind's innate adaptive intelligence; the value of developing the body/mind connection through intention and a "quiet mind"; and the benefit of "letting go" of thoughts, beliefs, and patterns that promote limitation.

After holistic wellness perspectives had become integral to my life, I wondered if cultivating my natural kinesthetic intelligence could help improve my golf game. Intrigued by this idea, I sought to discover how the joy of improvement might be found through the cultivation of instinctive abilities rather than reliance on instructions from others. Subsequently, over the years I devised a wide variety of instinct-awakening golf exercises for use as tools to tap into the innate kinesthetic intelligence of the body/mind, forty of which are included in this book.

These instinct-awakening golf exercises arose out of curiosity. I did not *try* to create them or *try* to find a method to help others awaken their kinesthetic intelligence to hit a golf ball. Rather, the exercises developed as a result of my experiences and an open mind—or "beginner's mind," a concept from Eastern philosophy that is addressed in chapter 3.

Learning to rely on *feel* to play golf seemed to require letting go of the sense of control inherent in visual dominance and instead learning to trust my kinesthetic intelligence to carry out my intentions—almost as if I had dropped my eyes into my body. Relying on the sensations in my body did indeed help me let go of the effort commonly generated by the conscious thinking mind and led me to discover the effortless flow characteristic of the natural workings of the body/mind.

My philosophy has always been to learn golf through observation—to be a "student of the game." My credentials come from playing, competing, and observing the game for more than fifty years, all the while achieving a growing awareness of how the body moves, learns, and follows the laws of nature. This, along with experiencing the holistic relationship between the body/mind's intelligence and the use of imagination and intention, has guided me to help golfers improve their golf game through discovery of their instinctive kinesthetic abilities. Shifting from "trying to beat others" to helping them discover their natural abilities has been a rewarding personal growth experience of unbounded joy.

Empowering the Golfer

How my "holistic" golf approach compares to conventional golf instruction is similar to how holistic wellness compares to conventional medicine. The holistic approach empowers the individual as a learner, while the conventional approach empowers the "expert" as the teacher. The holistic approach is internally focused, while the conventional approach is focused externally.

You don't need to have compromised physical senses to discover your body/mind intelligence. You only need an intention to explore. Then, while exploring you'll likely encounter a satisfying yet underutilized and underappreciated bodily sense deep within yourself. Think of it as your genius— or better yet, as your inner golfer. And regard the guidance in this book as a means for awakening your inner golfer.

Curiosity, combined with the intention to explore variations in grip, stance, swing, and the subtle senses without judgment or expectations, can take you beyond old, familiar patterns. Suddenly aware of deeper parts of yourself, you are likely to not only improve your golf game but also access previously unrecognized innate abilities. As you do, may you delight in many "aha!" moments of joy and discovery.

Introduction

We cannot teach people anything;
we can only help them discover it within themselves.

—Galileo Galilei

Awaken Your Inner Golfer is not a book that teaches you a method. It's a book of self-discovery that helps you learn, or reconnect with, what your body/mind already knows. It's about *fun* rather than *struggle*. It's about allowing rather than trying. It's about relaxing your mind and engaging your body to discover innate abilities rather than digesting external information. Welcome to exploration and discovery!

Feel cannot be taught . . . but it can be learned.

Your body/mind has been patiently waiting to be awakened and exercised. This you can accomplish by letting go of the dominance of your thinking, analytical mind, thereby allowing you to discover your unique instinctive abilities to perform movements effectively. In doing so, you will learn to play golf more from your subconscious mind than from your conscious mind. And if you explore the golf exercises regularly, who knows how else learning to trust your instincts may improve your life!

Your body/mind seeks your awareness and wants to serve you. It wants to free you from your conditioned mind. It wants to liberate you from the limitations of teachings. Your body/mind wants to bring you the joy of self-discovery through a connection with your senses of feel and instinct.

So much in today's world—computers, the Internet, technology, gadgets—encourages a connection with things and processes outside of ourselves. By contrast, this book encourages connections within ourselves, at once awakening the subtle senses and deepening the body/mind link. It promotes the integration of head and heart, mind and soul. It teaches you to trust your body's intelligence and to unlock those innate instincts that have been waiting to "come out and play."

The holistic nature of the golf exercises in particular helps to "sync up" your mind and your body, your conscious mind and subconscious mind, your left brain and right brain, and your mind's intention with your body's performance. Swinging a golf club, for instance, is primarily a right-brain function. Exploring the exercises is a balance of left- and right-brain functions. Your left brain analyzes an exercise, establishes an intention, and "hands it off" to your right brain to perform the movements. Thus practicing the swing exercises, as well as others, engages the whole brain.

Reflecting on the current level of participation in golf and many players' questionable enjoyment of the game, I can't help but wonder if a shift in consciousness might contribute to increased participation and enjoyment. I believe we may in fact be transitioning from concentrating on the analytical aspects of score and "par" to focusing on the sensory joy and satisfaction that come with hitting a golf ball effortlessly and playing a golf shot exactly as intended. We may be shifting from the ego's focus on results to the heart and soul's desire for deeper discovery. We may be evolving from "keeping score" to "awakening feelings."

I urge you to arrive at your own insights by exploring how the instinct-awakening exercises in chapter 7 impact your game. A score comes and goes, and in being attached to it we become only as "good" as our last score. But the sensory satisfaction of hitting a solid golf shot creates a deeper, more enduring memory in the body/mind. The experience of body and mind instinctively functioning in unison—intention meeting performance through fun, play, and self-discovery—may be what we are unconsciously yearning for in playing golf.

When we focus on the *process* of building feel, awakening instinct, and cultivating a deeper experience of sensory satisfaction, the *result* (score) just takes care of itself. This is what a serene life is about—enjoying the process rather than striving to achieve. It's about *being here* rather than *trying to get there*.

This book is designed to fit in your pocket so you can easily refer to the illustrations in chapter 5 and exercises in chapter 7 when you go to the range or practice area. You could explore the exercises without reading the preceding chapters, but you'll get the most benefit from them by first digesting the philosophy and the approach to building feel and awakening instinct. The exercises can help you tap into your limitless potential through immersion in the true nature of learning—through the joy and satisfaction resulting from trial and error, exploration and discovery.

Chapter 1

Kinesthetic Intelligence

*It is difficult to teach a motor skill by
telling someone what to do,
because the thing that must be done is a feeling,
a kinesthetic, wholly, subjective sensation.*

—Denise McCluggage, *The Centered Skier*

Tuning in to the Body/Mind Connection

Kinesthetic intelligence is the sense of bodily movement, balance, and coordination that occurs while performing motor skills. When utilized, this faculty enhances our ability to handle objects, such as golf clubs, skillfully for their intended purpose. It is an awareness of the union of mind and body, intention and movement. It's a form of "body knowing" awakened and developed through experience and adaptation.

Awareness of our kinesthetic intelligence is heightened each time we tune in to the links that exist between the mind and sensations in the body while performing movements. For this reason I use the term "kinesthetic intelligence" interchangeably with the word *feel*, which *Webster's New World Dictionary* defines as: "To be aware of through physical sensations."

I believe that in golf a sense of freedom beyond mechanics and technique allows us to express our unique kinesthetic intelligence. I further believe that each golfer has an instinctive ability to hit a golf ball. Most professional golfers begin developing kinesthetic intelligence at a young age and continue to exercise the neural/muscular connections involved in hitting a golf ball through regular practice and play. Many others start golf later in life or experience interruptions in developing their kinesthetic intelligence, and thus may be led to believe more in analytical approaches or instruction by "experts." In such instances, kinesthetic intelligence may remain temporarily dormant.

When the body/mind connection involved in complex motor activities such as golf swings is severely underutilized— meaning the neural/muscular pathways have not been used on a regular basis—golf can seem very difficult for adults to master. Fortunately, awareness of these connections can be awakened.

> *The reason why golf is so difficult is that you have to*
> *learn it and play it through your senses.*
> *You must be mindful but not thoughtful as you swing.*
> *You must not think or reflect;*
> *you must feel what you have to do.*
>
> —Percy Boomer, *On Learning Golf*

Improved performance is a natural by-product of awakening kinesthetic intelligence. You don't learn about *your* golf swing by reading an instruction manual or listening to directions; you learn about it through tuning in to your instinctual abilities while swinging a golf club. The exercises in chapter

7 were specifically designed to reacquaint golfers with their instinctual abilities—and their childlike joy in playing golf.

The exercises are "experiential," providing instinct-stimulating movements, visualizations, and golf swing explorations that help quiet the mind and awaken the body. They facilitate learning what you already know. While performing them, you'll be "educating" your hands and feeling the connection between your hands and the clubface. You'll be *learning how to learn*. Research shows that learning through self-discovery has greater permanence in the body/mind than attempting to learn through instruction. There's no need to try to accomplish anything with the exercises—just have fun!

Possibly the most common conditioned thought pattern in assessing the results of hitting a golf ball poorly is, "What did I do wrong?" This implies that your conscious mind could figure out what went "wrong" in the one and a half seconds of a golf swing and direct your body to follow its instructions to "do it right" the next time. But your conscious mind can't instruct your body to carry out the complex movements of a golf swing, especially in the one and a half seconds it takes to make a swing. It is your subconscious mind that's responsible for your body's movements. Perfecting your motor skills therefore requires stimulating the subtle senses in the body/mind and recognizing the *feel* of an effective swing, resulting in authentic learning. Your instincts are perfectly innate and innately perfect.

> *If you can align with your subtle senses,*
> *you will have found the secret of touch.*
>
> —Deepak Chopra, *Golf for Enlightenment*

Putting Kinesthetic Intelligence to Work

As you practice awareness of "being in your body" while working with the golf exercises, you'll not only learn to feel the sensations of movement that produce pure impact with the golf ball but you'll ingrain the sensation of "pure impact" deeper and deeper into your subconscious mind. In time you'll be able to recall the *feel* of pure impact to produce consistent mechanics.

Once a movement such as a golf swing is learned, the *feel* of it is stored permanently in the part of your brain responsible for motor skills—often called "muscle memory," or "motor memory." That is why, in the exercises and elsewhere, it is possible to recall the feel of pure impact and allow your body/mind to perform the mechanics needed to reproduce that feel. Trust it!

*You will simply alter your swing unconsciously in response
to your feeling of what will produce the shot you want.
In other words, control of your shots has now been placed
outside of your conscious mind and will.*

—Percy Boomer, *On Learning Golf*

Conventional golf instruction usually tells or shows us what to do and what not to do. In response, the conscious mind attempts to comply by initiating a series of fixes and corrections. This approach, although traditional, is contrary to how we as human beings learn, especially when it comes to complex motor skills such as golf swings. As children, we learn to walk by engaging not only the brain but also the body and nervous system operating in full collaboration. I suggest that stimulation of the subtle senses in the body/mind is also the best way to learn the feel of your unique golf swing.

The only source of knowledge is experience.

—Albert Einstein

The golf exercises in chapter 7 won't necessarily change your swing, but there's a good chance they will help you find your most effective swing. Indeed, this book is not about the *right way* to swing a golf club; it's about discovering *your way*. There's no *right*, just *insight*! Your swing is within you; putting kinesthetic intelligence to work simply facilitates the opening of pathways to potential so you can experience excellence.

To perform a learned motor skill efficiently, we must quiet our conscious minds and establish the intention to activate muscle memory. Intention is the "fuel" that ignites the "engine" of the motor system stored in the subconscious mind. The integration of the conscious mind's intention and the subconscious mind's ability to carry out the movement is something that can't be explained but can only be experienced.

What we learn to do, we learn by doing.

—Aristotle

Chapter 2
Discovering Unconscious Competency, Releasing Fear, and Letting Go

Trusting the unfamiliar is always frightening at first, but experience will prove that relinquishing ego control is a matter not of giving up something but of shifting to a control system that is infinitely more sophisticated and capable.

—W. Timothy Gallwey, *The Inner Game of Golf*

Discovering Our Unconscious Competency

A vitally important way to learn golf or improve golf performance is to welcome expression of the subconscious mind. The conscious mind governs controlled behavior, such as thinking and evaluating, and the subconscious mind governs automatic behavior, like movement and internal bodily functions. The conscious mind thinks; the subconscious mind *senses*.

Fun, play, and self-discovery stimulates awareness of this deeper dimension of the self. It does so by freeing our kinesthetic intelligence to direct the motor skills needed to carry out the conscious mind's intentions, manifesting our unconscious competency.

As we become adults, the conscious mind often seems to interfere with our golf performance. Could the solution be to play and have fun with golf? Might having fun with the golf exercises quiet the conscious mind and allow the subconscious kinesthetic intelligence responsible for directing motor skills the opportunity to be "heard"?

The body/mind can play a beautiful symphony through a golf swing. The noise produced by constant thinking, however, too often drowns out the music by causing us to lose contact with our unconscious competency.

Swapping Fear for Freedom

Another factor that interferes with our golf performance is fear. In releasing fear we can uncover our innocence—and inner sense of ourselves—layered over by doubts and worries of what others think or how we judge ourselves. Children don't fear hitting a few "clunkers" on the range or the golf course. They intuitively know that bungled shots are just part of learning; without consciously thinking or judging, they trust their instinctive adaptive intelligence.

Could it be that true control appears when we are freed to take such risks and make mistakes in hitting a golf ball? Can the freedom to make a mistake free us of our minds' fears, which sometimes impede our movements? In my work with novice and experienced golfers, I've found that in both instances freedom from fear improves golf performance because it facilitates flow.

Flow is *present moment awareness*—attending to each moment as it streams, unobstructed, into the next without feeling a need to *try* or *accomplish*. When one is in this state, the extraordinary has an opportunity to "show up."

If you fear hitting a "bad shot" or "losing your swing," you may especially benefit from the freedom generated by the golf exercises. After all, judging or labeling a shot as "bad" while exploring these exercises will impede flow, causing you to reject the potential for adaptive learning, which is the natural way human beings learn. Stimulating the body/mind's kinesthetic intelligence, on the other hand, will facilitate flow, counteracting the "paralysis" produced by fear.

Letting Go to Access What We Already Know

If the intellect is engaged during a motion,
the body will not be free.

—STEVEN YELLIN, *THE FLUID MOTION FACTOR*

We access what we already know—our unconscious competency— simply by letting go of old unproductive patterns and beliefs. Just reflecting on the term "letting go" can reveal whether we have a tendency to hold on to ingrained physical and mental routines that are no longer productive.

Unproductive patterns and beliefs are limiting, separating us from a sense of our inherent power, instinctive abilities, and adaptive intelligence. Such routines have the same effect in life as in golf—although, as an associate once said, "Well, golf *is* life!" In golf and in life, we rely on the programming of the conscious mind to find solutions to problems from outside ourselves when actually the subconscious mind has the answers, which we can find through quiet awareness.

The more we loosen the boundaries around our instinctive abilities, the more we experience the power of our potential and ultimately move beyond the mind's interference. A good example of this dynamic can be seen in efforts taken to balance the left and right brain hemispheres. The analytical left brain tries to analyze, understand, and make sense of things—that's its job. But because its influence has become too pervasive in today's analytical-oriented society, individuals seek balance by stimulating the imagination, spatial ability, and creativity of the right brain.

Letting go of unproductive patterns and beliefs implies letting go of the mind's need to control, instruct, manage, analyze, build itself up, solve problems, and *be needed*. It's about trust—trusting your instincts, trusting the innate ability of your subconscious mind, trusting *what you already know*! It's about relaxing—letting go of the tension produced by the mind, whether out of fear, effort, competitiveness, self-consciousness, or another ingrained pattern or belief. The mind's obsession with control can be so exhausting that letting go may lead to an immediate sense of flow!

The golf exercises help antidote the habit of allowing the mind to direct the body's motions. They do this by fostering a deepening awareness of the bodily sensations involved in swinging and hitting a golf ball. Although letting go of the mind's domination is not always easy, and it could even feel somewhat "painful" to step away from this illusion of control, real power comes from a letting go into your innate instincts.

Letting go is also about opening up. When we let go of old patterns and beliefs, we open to something new. When we empty ourselves of external conditioning, we increase our receptivity to internal connections and realities—including our potential magic and innate wisdom.

> *Control is an illusion*
> *And causes confusion.*
> *Pathways open through a "letting go"*
> *To the genius of what you already know.*

Chapter 3

Play, "Beginner's Mind," and Mindfulness

There is a great deal of evidence that the road to mastery of any subject is guided by play.

—Stuart Brown, MD, *Play*

Play

Play is movement. Movement facilitates present moment awareness. When we tune in to the present moment, we adapt and learn.

Play feeds not only our mobility and adaptability but also our flexibility, versatility, and tranquility. In addition, play fosters the development of instincts. As children, we developed our instincts through play and, in many instances, went on to become instinctive players—in sports, games, even music—as opposed to contemplative players. As adults, we can consciously choose to follow "the way of a child" in order to reawaken our instincts.

Golf practice can help us do this by reestablishing a body/mind connection that may have been temporarily lost when we stopped playing games and having fun—when we stopped bike riding, skipping rope, playing catch or hopscotch, or shooting hoops. When we cease using the body to learn and succumb to Adultitis, it keeps us beholden to the mind in a society obsessed with results and productivity.

> *In the learning is the fun.*
> *In the fun is the freedom.*
> *In the freedom is the performance.*
> *In the performance is the satisfaction.*

The seriousness and competitiveness so rampant in today's outcome-oriented society inhibits, and even shuts down, expressions of playfulness to avoid judgment, criticism, or ridicule. Fortunately, we can reclaim our playful nature by releasing any attachment to such responses and making golf practice our play and play our golf practice.

> *The creation of something new*
> *is not accomplished by the intellect*
> *but by the play instinct*
> *acting from inner necessity.*
>
> —CARL JUNG

Anyone who considers it "childlike" to play and have fun is right. Anyone who thinks they are too old, too conditioned, or too "mature" to adopt the way of a child might benefit from reevaluating this pattern of thought. Playing and having fun are what keep us learning and keep us young—in body, mind, and spirit!

> *We don't stop playing because we grow old;*
> *we grow old because we stop playing.*
>
> —GEORGE BERNARD SHAW

"Beginner's Mind"

It is important in golf, as in life, to have an open mind and, even better, to have a "beginner's mind." In Eastern philosophy, beginner's mind is one that has been emptied of conditioned ideas, concepts, techniques, and methods. Essential elements of beginner's mind are innocence and wonder, which allow the individual to see what shows up while investigating a situation.

In the beginner's mind there are many possibilities;
in the expert's mind there are few.

—SHUNRYU SUZUKI

Beginner's mind is also receptive rather than active, and quiet rather than noisy. While a noisy mind is caught up in conditioned thoughts from the past about how to swing a golf club or how to hit a golf ball, a quiet mind is able to fully experience the present and reveal something new about these motions.

Improving your golf game, as well as learning to play, calls for a mind that is receptive and quiet—open, eager, and free of preconceptions. Then, whether it is investigating a skill for the first time or the hundredth time, something new is bound to arise from the depths of the subconscious mind, where imagination, instinct, intuition, and insight reside.

Mindfulness

Mindfulness, also essential to awakening one's inner golfer, entails approaching the sport with a nonjudgmental mind to see what shows up beyond the person's preconceived ideas and perceptions. In their book *Fully Present*, scientist Susan Smalley and mindfulness teacher Diana Winston describe mindfulness as "the art of observing your physical, emotional, and mental experiences with deliberate, open, and curious attention."[1]

To be mindful is to be aware. Mindfulness can be described as "present moment awareness" or "conscious awareness," in which consciousness represents the totality of the person's thoughts and feelings. In bringing this state of awareness to our practice of golf, we are likely to experience being fully present, with heightened physical sensations and a calm, focused mind. In time, mindfulness may lead us to discover that *we are more than our mind*—that our mind is a servant to our heart and that our heart revels in its newfound freedom from the contraints imposed by fear, judgment, and control.

Commenting on "conscious practices," Smalley and Winston state, "When someone is in the zone, or flow, there is a sense of losing oneself in the experience, forgetting about the 'I' doing the exercise, and becoming fully immersed in the experience. . . . It is an alternative state of consciousness where the action arises while the 'I' rests."[2]

Practicing mindfulness while exploring the golf exercises in chapter 7 can carry over not only to your time on the range or the golf course but to your immersion in everyday activities as well. Cultivating a nonjudgmental mind can have vast ramifications, allowing you to see what shows up—in golf and in life.

Golf is also a game to teach you about the messages from within, about the subtle voices of the body-mind.

—MICHAEL MURPHY, *GOLF IN THE KINGDOM*

Chapter 4

Personal Rhythm, Visualization, and Imagination

Effortlessness is synonymous with good rhythm.

—MICHAEL MCTEIGUE

THE KEYS TO THE EFFORTLESS GOLF SWING

Personal Rhythm

Rhythm—not grip, posture, or mechanics—is the soul of the golf swing. Golfers must find their personal rhythm through trial and error, failure and success, exploration and discovery. It can't be defined by, or taught through, words. It can't be shown. It can't be thought into being. Personal rhythm is experienced as a *feel*. It's a *flow* in the body/mind accessed through a deep sense of the movement involved.

Not only is rhythm the soul of the golf swing but the golfer's hands are the heartbeat of the swing. Conventional golf instruction often focuses on use of the big muscles of the body in swinging a golf club and minimizes the importance of the hands. But the feel in the hands is what gets communicated to the brain! Our hands convey to our brains both the *feel* of pure impact and the *feel* of clunkers.

In other words, the mechanics for pure impact originate in your body/mind's ability to unconsciously discern muscular messages felt through your hands. Similar to how your heartbeat influences your bodily rhythm, your hands influence the rhythm of your golf swing. Several of the golf exercises in chapter 7 will help educate your hands to discover that rhythm.

Visualization and Imagination

We visualize and imagine movement when we think about playing sports or performing other physical activities. We "see" images in our mind's eye at such times. The subconscious mind is designed to work with images. In fact, research shows that the subconscious mind does not distinguish between what is real and what is imagined. Our nervous system and muscles respond exactly the same whether we imagine a movement or actually make the movement.

Consequently, it is very helpful to use visualization and imagination when developing or improving golf skills. To engage the subconscious mind in this endeavor, the images need not be pictures; they can be feelings, such as the feeling of pure impact while hitting a golf ball.

When we imagine a feeling of pure impact, our instinctive kinesthetic intelligence almost instantly develops neural/muscular messages to produce that feeling. As Dr. Joseph Parent states in his book *Zen Golf*, "When you establish an image of what you intend to do, the body will fulfill it. The clearer the image, the more likely your body will produce it….The best swing thought is actually an image, not a conceptual thought."[1]

Remember, images are what instruct the body.
Talk to yourself in words if you want to,
but be sure that the words are translated into
sight images, sound images, feeling images.

—Denise McCluggage, *The Centered Skier*

The more you practice visualization and imagination, the better equipped you will be to fuel the motor system of your body/mind to produce that feeling. What you "see" is what you get.

Chapter 5

Foundations of Effective Grip and Posture

We cannot get away from the fact that golf is basically a matter of grip and set-up.

—John Jacobs, *Practical Golf*

Just as a builder needs a solid foundation to construct a sturdy building, a golfer requires reliable foundations to perform movements capable of producing a dynamic golf swing. Following are guidelines for establishing those foundations.

Effective Grip

The basic factor in all good golf is the grip. Get it right, and all other progress follows.

—Tommy Armour, *How to Play Your Best Golf All the Time*

In my personal and coaching experience, the most common root cause of "swing flaws" is an ineffective grip. In fact, grip seems to be an overlooked aspect of conventional golf instruction. In his insightful book *Rethinking Golf*, Chuck Hogan states, "So much time is needed to devote to this skill that virtually all traditional instruction has learned to skip over the proper hold for fear that the student will get bored and frustrated because they can't 'hit balls.'"[1] In instances of an ineffective grip, the body's kinesthetic intelligence attempts to compensate. This works sometimes, but it takes energy and effort, and stifles natural instincts.

An effective grip is one that *feels* the best and, more importantly, *performs* the best. You know you have an effective grip when you can feel your hands working in unison with each other and the rotation of your body to carry the energy of that rotation to the golf club and when you can feel the clubface opening on the backswing, naturally squaring to the target at the ball and closing after impact—*without manipulation or control by your hands*. An effective grip creates a link with the golf club to swing the weight of the clubhead, through centrifugal force, with speed and consistency.

Placement of the hands on the golf grip is the nerve center of the swing. The hands transmit sensations and information to and from the body/mind. The hands do not make the golf club swing, but they do instinctively react to the movement of the torso and arms. When the hands are placed on the golf grip in an optimum position, they instinctively carry out the body's instructions to swing the golf club effectively. In this way, your swing, pitch, or chip can become automatic and effortless.

Therefore, it's very important to begin with a foundation of effective grip so your hands, wrists, and arms can instinctively carry out the rotation of your torso. This natural rotation, combined with the hinging and unhinging of your hands and wrists, allows you to leverage the momentum of the weight of the clubhead for power and control.

While there's not one correct grip, there are specific anatomical principles underlying the positioning of the hands on the golf grip to maintain control of the clubhead while hitting a golf ball. Think about holding a toothbrush, a fork, or a hammer. Is there a *correct* way to place your hands and fingers on each implement or is there an *effective* way to hold the implement so your body can best use it for its designed purpose?

It takes considerable attention and conscious effort to place the hands on the golf grip effectively, and even more effort to change an ingrained ineffective grip as there is usually strong resistance to changing any familiar pattern. But such change may be necessary in order to have a powerful and consistent golf swing. The good news is that your conscious attention to this connection of body and golf club will promote an effortless and dynamic golf swing and deliver the joy and satisfaction of pure impact.

The hold of the golf club (how you form your hands on the club)
is both the most important and most complicated fundamental
in learning to swing and strike the ball efficiently.
Therefore, any lack of clarity and precision
as you imprint this activity in your brain
will have a huge impact on your future proficiency.

—Chuck Hogan, *Rethinking Golf*

The three basic traditional grips (from a right-handed golfer's perspective) are as follows:

1. Ten-finger grip (also called "baseball grip")—all ten fingers on the grip.
2. Overlap grip—the right pinky finger curled over and around the middle knuckle of the left index finger.
3. Interlock grip—the right pinky finger interlocked between

the left index finger and the middle finger. (The word *interlock* is somewhat misleading since it's actually a "hook" of the right pinky finger around the base of the left index finger.)

Most golfers place their hands on the golf grip using one of these traditional grips while they are in an address position with the clubhead on the ground in front of them. This can be counterproductive because the common intuitive response is to grip the golf club in the palm of the left hand. If all we wanted was to hold the clubhead on the ground in a static position, that would be a useful intuitive response. But we want to swing the weight of the clubhead in an arc around the body, using the connection of body and golf club to produce a centrifugal force that gives the clubhead sufficient speed to hit the golf ball solidly. This requires having the golf club *leveraged in the fingers* so arms, wrists, and hands can rotate and hinge naturally, according to their anatomical function and design.

Following are six foundational exercises to help stimulate the feeling of an effective grip. With apologies to left-handed golfers, all exercises and references in this book are described from a right-handed golfer's perspective. Ironically, left-handed golfers may build even more skill by "being in the body" to reverse this orientation.

Foundational Exercise 1

Cradling a Pen Securely in All Five Fingers

In your left hand, cradle a pen securely in all five fingers. Feel the leverage while gently squeezing with your thumb and index finger, as if gradually urging the ink out the tip of the pen, as shown in figure 5.1. Repeat the exercise using your right hand.

Figure 5.1

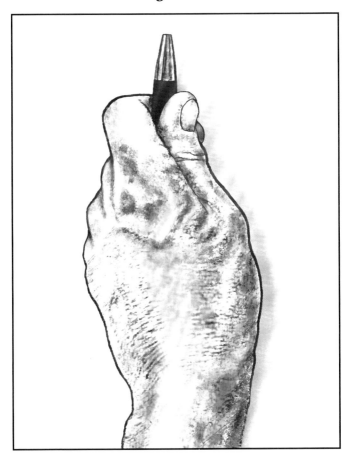

Your grip on the golf club will not be this forceful. The exercise is simply to help you experience how leveraged in the fingers *feels*.

Foundational Exercise 2

Twirling a Weight at the End of a String

Imagine a weight at the end of a string attached to a pen. First with your left hand and then with your right hand cradle the pen in all five fingers (see Foundational Exercise 1 on page 39) and twirl your hand to make the imaginary weight move fast in a vertical circle in front of you. Twirl each hand first to the right and then to the left, feeling the freedom of movement in your hands and wrists.

Next, to experience the feel of an ineffective grip, hold the pen in the *palm* of each hand, along the lifeline leading to your wrist. Twirl your hand and the imaginary weight, and feel the restriction of motion in your hands and wrists.

Having freedom of movement in your hands and wrists is the goal when placing your hands on the golf grip. It will help you to swing the weight of the clubhead just like the imaginary weight at the end of a string.

Foundational Exercise 3

Placing the Right Index Finger in the Left Hand

You can practice an effective grip position with your left hand at any time by bringing your hands out in front of your chest and placing your right index finger in your left hand, as shown in figure 5.2. Then, as illustrated in figure 5.3,

Figure 5.2

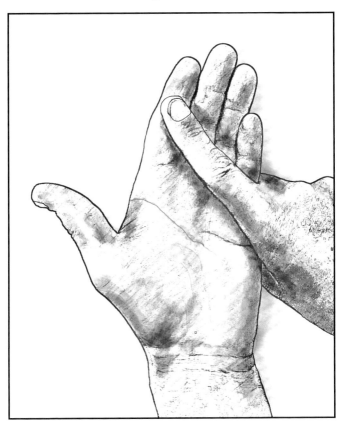

gently wrap the fingers of your left hand around the right index finger, feeling the tip of the left thumb and the middle pad of the left index finger cradling the tip and fingernail of the right index finger just as they cradle the golf grip. While holding your hands in front of your chest in this position, you'll see the top of the middle knuckle of your left index finger and the two big knuckles of your left middle and index fingers.

Figure 5.3

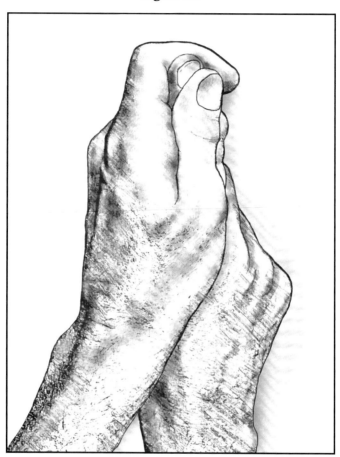

Foundational Exercise 4

Placing the Left Hand on the Golf Grip

Having the golf grip leveraged in the fingers allows your hands to hinge, rotate, and function dynamically, as they are anatomically designed to do. This takes some practice, patience, and awareness, but it will pay off dearly.

Stand up with your feet about hip width apart. With the shaft leaning toward the target and parallel to the target line, rest the clubhead on the ground midway between your feet and even with your toe line, with the bottom, or "leading edge," of the clubface parallel to your toe line and the target line, as shown in figure 5.4.

With your left arm fully extended to the side of your left leg, allow the golf grip—about one-half inch below the top of the grip—to gently rest in the fingers of your open left hand, as shown in figure 5.5.

Figure 5.4

Figure 5.5

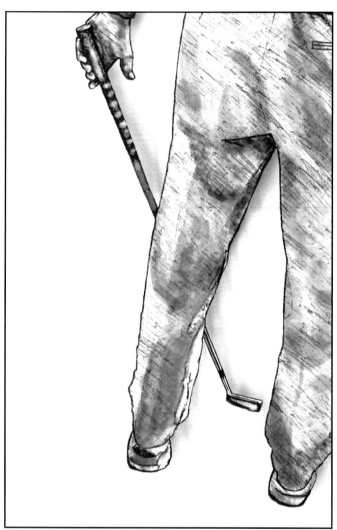

Then, with your left arm fully extended in a natural man-
ner, wrap your fingers around the grip about one-half inch
below the top of the grip, with the fingernail of your left

thumb facing the side of your left buttock, as shown in figure 5.6. Looking down, you should see all four big knuckles of your left hand and a concave hinge in your left wrist, and feel a slight trigger position of your left index finger—the same feel as cradling the pen in all five fingers of the left hand.

Figure 5.6

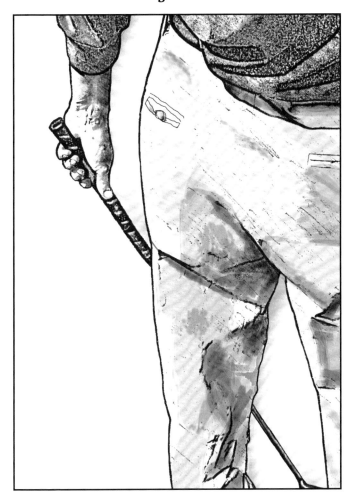

If you then hold the golf club vertically out in front of you, as shown in figure 5.7, you should see the hinge in your left wrist and observe the top of the middle knuckle of your left index finger and the two big knuckles of your left middle and index fingers, with your left thumb at approximately a one o'clock position on the grip. Keep this hinge in your left wrist when you bring the golf club to an address position.

Figure 5.7

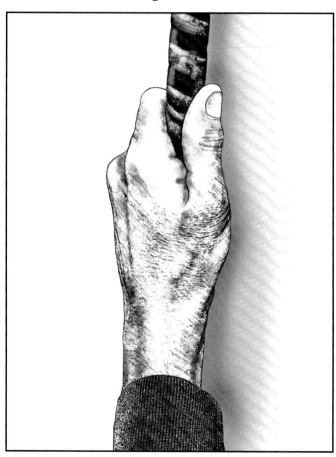

Still holding the golf club vertically out in front of you, open the fingers of your left hand. The position of the grip in your left hand should appear similar to that illustrated in figure 5.8.

Figure 5.8

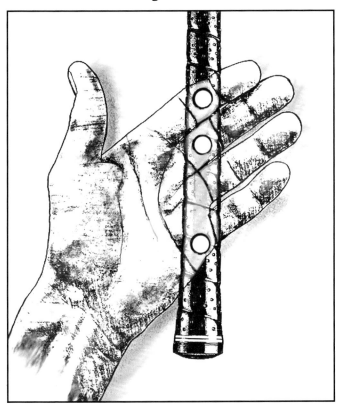

Foundational Exercise 5

Placing the Right Hand on the Golf Grip

While holding the golf club leveraged in the fingers of the left hand and extended out in front of you perpendicular to your body at waist level, put your right hand out as if you were about to shake hands with someone at the end of the golf club, as shown in figure 5.9.

Then, while keeping the same angle and position of your right hand, slide it onto the grip to meet your left hand so the lifeline of your right hand that leads to your wrist rests over the middle of your left thumb. There will be a slight downward pressure from this "slot" in your right hand that fits perfectly over your left thumb.

Gently wrap all ten fingers around the grip, with the top of your right thumb resting gently but securely on the grip at approximately an eleven o'clock position and little or no gap between the base of your thumb and index fingers. Your right index finger should be in a slight trigger position with a small gap between the middle and index fingers. This helps support the weight of the golf club.

If you hold the golf club vertically in front of you and open your right hand, the position of the golf grip will look similar to the one illustrated in figure 5.10. If you prefer to use an overlap or interlock grip rather than a ten-finger grip, move your right hand up without rotating it and overlap or interlock your right pinky finger, as described on pages 37 and 38.

Although professionals may grip the golf club with the clubhead on the ground in an address position, following this grip exercise before every shot will help you ingrain the feeling of an effective grip so that it becomes automatic. Your grip will become instinctive and will allow you to swing as you are anatomically designed to do.

Figure 5.9

Figure 5.10

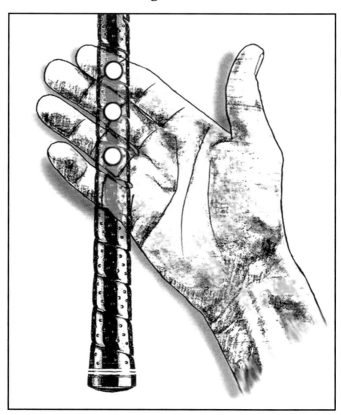

Foundational Exercise 6

A Neutral Grip

With your hands on the golf club in an address position, notice that the creases formed between the thumb and index fingers of each hand—sometimes referred to as the "V's"—point to approximately the same spot between your neck and your right shoulder. This is a neutral grip, shown in figure 5.11. Having the V's of each hand pointing to the same spot allows your hands to move in a complementary rather than oppositional way.

Although there is no one grip that fits everyone, the neutral grip should give you the feeling of an effective grip that allows your hands, wrists, and forearms to work in unison with one another, the golf club, and your body's movement. If you need to, you can tweak the grip to a "weak" or "strong" position tailored to your physiology and unique movement,

Figure 5.11

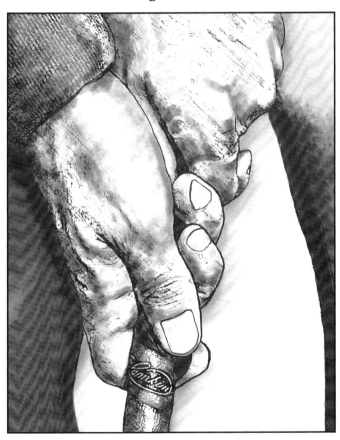

making certain that the V of each hand points to the same place. To try a "weak" position, rotate both hands to the left so that your left thumb is at about a twelve o'clock position on the grip and the V's of both hands point toward your neck. To try a "strong" position, rotate both hands to the right so that your left thumb is at about a two o'clock position and the V's are pointing to your right shoulder.

Congratulations! You have just learned how to place your hands on the golf club effectively. By contrast, figures 5.12, 5.13, and 5.14 illustrate ineffective grips in the left hand.

Figure 5.12

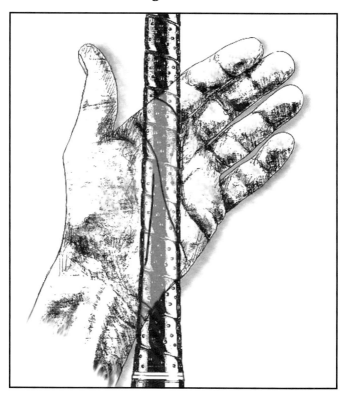

Figure 5.13

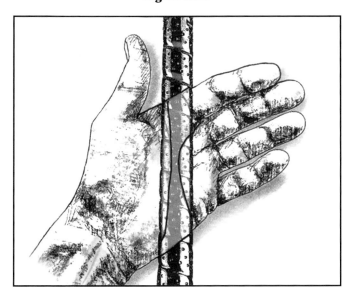

Figure 5.14

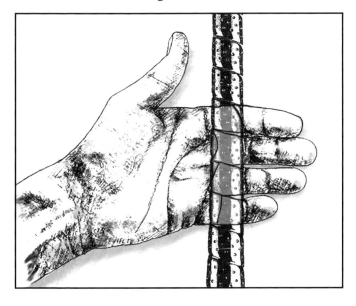

Effective Posture

Effective posture allows your torso to rotate around your spine easily, instinctively, and naturally, providing the origin of movement and energy for swinging a golf club. In his book *Zen Golf*, Dr. Joseph Parent, describing the origin of movement in the body, notes: "In the martial arts and similar mind-body traditions of the East, the body's 'center of gravity' is the source from which all movements and energy flow. It is located a few inches below the navel, in the center of the torso. In the Japanese martial arts it is called the *hara*, in Chinese traditions like tai chi it is called the *dantien*, and in Tibetan Yoga it is called the *chojung*."[2] In the golf exercises, the "center of balance" and "origin of movement" are referred to as your core.

Practicing the foundation of effective posture will help you learn the *feel* of the pivot of your body while swinging the golf club. By originating pivot and movement from your core, you will be able to trust that your intention to hit a golf ball solidly in a specific direction and for a particular distance will be carried out by the instinctive kinesthetic intelligence of your body. And you'll be likely to gain a greater awareness of this origin of movement in the connection of your feet to the ground.

Foundational Exercise 7 is designed to help you feel effective posture through awakening your body's instinctive kinesthetic intelligence. The body learns from experience and awakens through feel and sensations; by contrast, it can get somewhat paralyzed in response to verbal commands and instructions.

Foundational Exercise 7

Posture

Everybody's frame is different. To *feel* the right posture for you, the one that seems natural and comfortable, follow the sequence of this exercise without a golf club at first.

1. Stand normally.

2. Make a small move as if you were about to sit on a high stool behind you, as illustrated in figure 5.15.

3. Look at an imaginary golf ball on the ground at address.

4. Gently press the sides of your hands into the creases of your thighs, feeling your tailbone dropping down very gently toward the ground. *Feel* how the creases are "drawn in" and the resulting sense of balance and stability.

5. a. *Feel* like you have roots growing into the ground from the bottoms of your feet. Alternate lifting your left and right toes ten times to confirm your sense of balance.

   b. *Feel* the centerline from your toes to your heels in each foot.

6. a. Experiment with the width of your stance in relation to the width of your hips and shoulders by sensing how different widths *feel*. Move your body as you try stances of different widths, and sense when your movement *feels* balanced and coordinated with the least amount of strain. You want to feel ready on your feet to initiate and coordinate movement with balance.

   b. Experiment with the flare, or angles, of your feet. Find a position that is comfortable and allows your body to freely pivot back and forth through your swing.

Figure 5.15

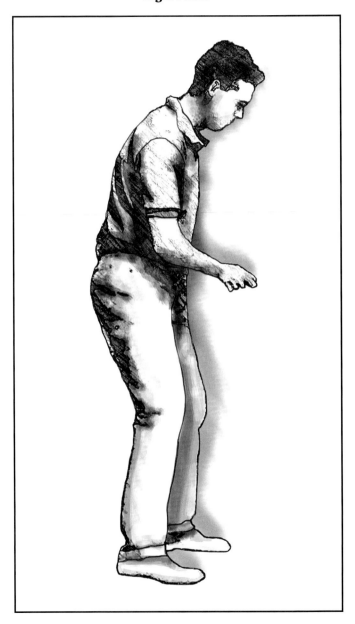

7. Place your hands together, right hand lower than left, as if on the grip of a golf club, addressing the ball. Notice how your right shoulder naturally drops lower than your left shoulder because your right hand is lower than your left hand on the grip of the golf club. *Feel* how your spine tilts slightly to the right, which provides stability when hitting the golf ball.

8. As shown in figure 5.16, if you look straight down in this balanced address position you should notice the following:

   • The front of your knees over the middle of your feet

   • Your hips over your heels

   • Your hands and the front of your shoulders just outside your toes

   • Your eyes just outside your hands

   • Your arms extended but relaxed, hanging from your shoulders, with your inner elbows facing more outward toward the golf ball than inward toward each other

   • Your shoulders relaxed, free of tension

9. Bring your awareness to the triangle formed by your hands, arms, and an imaginary line from shoulder to shoulder, as shown in figure 5.17. You will "turn the triangle" back to begin the backswing and then forward for the forward swing, a movement often referred to as "turning the triangle." The triangle is not rigid. Your arms and hands should be relaxed enough for your wrists and elbows to instinctively bend and hinge at the appropriate time to swing the weight of the clubhead.

Figure 5.16

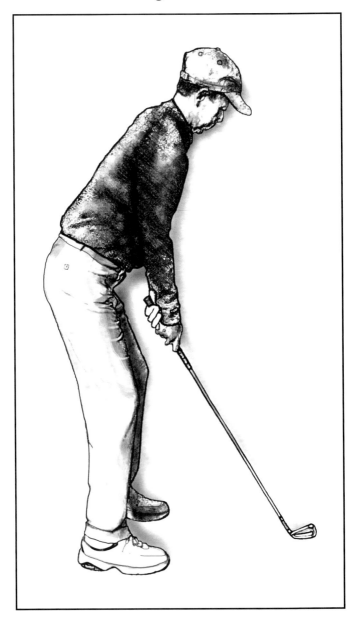

Figure 5.17

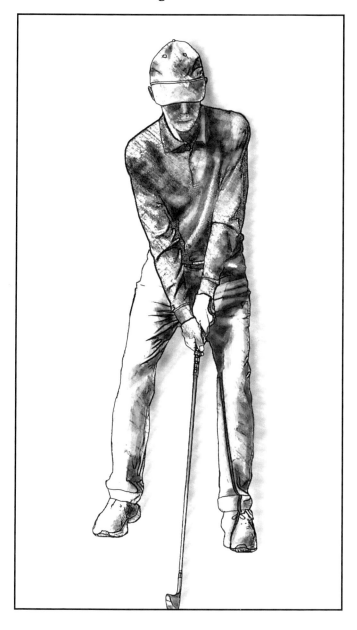

Once you are familiar with these seven foundational exercises and able to *feel* the posture and grip that are most effective for you, your golf game will quickly improve. Further advances will follow as you engage with the variety of golf exercises in chapter 7 to help awaken your body/mind's adaptive instincts.

Chapter 6

Guide to the Instinct-Awakening Golf Exercises

*During these times when judgment is withheld,
analyzation is suspended and we enter into
the realm of pure play,
we find that we are without limits.*

—CHUCK HOGAN, *RETHINKING GOLF*

The exercises described in chapter 7 are intended to provide a deep learning experience to improve your golf game through the natural way that we learn—through play and fun, exploration and discovery. With each one, I suggest that you begin by focusing on chip/pitch shots and half-swing full shots of fifty to one hundred yards with a pitching wedge (PW), which has more versatility than a sand or gap wedge. The versatility of the PW will allow you to tap in to your natural adaptive instincts.

Research has shown that full swings at high speed do not allow the brain enough time to change, so it will continue the patterns it has previously experienced. The chip/pitch and half-swing full shots, on the other hand, will give your brain the time it needs to form new neural/muscular patterns for improved performance.

This distinction leads to a question: Why don't most golfers practice their short game? I believe that not having a grip that allows for the development of delicate "touch-and-feel shots" may be a primary reason for this, and not knowing what to practice or how to practice may be secondary reasons. Consequently, many golfers assume there's a mystique associated with technique for short-game shots, leading them to feel intimidated, fearful of making "mistakes," and dissatisfied. In effect, most golfers don't practice their short game because it's been no fun!

Exploring the exercises first through the chip/pitch and half-swing full shots will help you develop *feel* in your hands, which will assist you in finding your personal rhythm. Developing your feel and personal rhythm through short shots will infuse the experience with fun and satisfaction, inspiring you to improve your short game.

After successfully hitting a solid short shot while practicing any of the exercises, ask yourself, "What did that *feel* like in my body and in my hands? What felt *different* or *new*?" Gaining awareness in this way will help strengthen your body/mind link and automatically transfer to your long game.

Practice Tips

To optimize your learning experiences while performing the golf exercises, consider implementing the following practice tips.

- Since your hands are the connection between the clubface and your body/mind, practice the exercises without a golf glove, as this will stimulate your sense of feel. Also experiment using a ten-finger grip to build feel.

- If you are hitting off grass turf, give yourself "good lies" sitting on top of the grass because the purpose of the exercises is not only to learn the feel of pure impact but to build on that success. As your body's kinesthetic intelligence increases and your sense of feel matures, you'll be fully capable of adapting to the "imperfect lies" sitting down in the grass or in the rough encountered on the golf course.

- Unless an exercise refers to focusing on a specific target, do the exercise in a spacious area— such as a driving range, field, or large chipping/pitching area—with an expansive target area so that your mind doesn't get caught up in "resultitis." The results will come as you stop seeking them.

- Remain aware of what you are *feeling* rather than trying to accomplish something. Trust that the feel will convert to effective mechanics without effort or interference from your mind. Notice the quality of the results when you do an exercise for the sake of experience versus when you do it to achieve results.

While exploring the exercises, you'll be accessing progressively deeper levels of instinctive kinesthetic intelligence and gaining greater sensitivity to feel. Though I cannot tell you or show you how to swing a golf club, through the exercises you'll discover the technique and mechanics that work for you and be able to identify your most effective swing when you feel it.

Progressive by Design

The exercises are progressive in nature, building on one another. The more often you practice them, the more you'll awaken your body/mind's instinctive kinesthetic intelligence and the stronger it will become. You'll be transforming your engagement in the game from *trying* to *knowing*, and from *struggling* to *flowing*!

Mixing a variety of the exercises on any day will keep your instincts alert and ready to respond, if not "show off." Any time you have a "show-off" moment, acknowledge your subconscious mind, which responds well to affirmation and gratitude. It may respond by giving you increasingly more "aha!" moments since it loves playfulness.

When practicing any of the exercises, especially those you struggle with, "talk" to your body and your subconscious. Ask your body, "How can you produce pure impact with this exercise?" Then *trust* in your instinctive kinesthetic intelligence to come through with the answer!

After a practice session with the exercises, regardless of the results, your body/mind will process the experience by integrating the feel of the successful shots into your neural/muscular system. It will also create adaptations in your neural/muscular system for the unsuccessful shots so you can experience greater success with them the next time you practice.

Patience Precipitates Potential

Exploring the golf exercises involves learning how to practice and practicing how to learn, both of which take patience. You'll hit some clunkers and make some blunders, but there are no mistakes—only opportunities for learning.

You either can allow the clunkers to block you from further stimulating your kinesthetic intelligence or use them to help access your untapped genius. Alternatively, you may interpret your mind's conditioned reaction to a challenging exercise as "I *can't* do this one" but soon come to the startling awareness that the reaction is actually "I *won't* do this one" and then change your mind.

At some unexpected point in your exploration of the exercises, practice will no longer be a chore or a bore. Neither frustrating, discouraging, nor enraging, it will be experienced as the learning opportunity it actually is. Satisfaction will come from patiently allowing yourself the freedom to make some "mistakes" and then adapting and learning from them.

It is important to realize that the purpose of the exercises is not to *get* somewhere. The purpose is rather to *be* somewhere—present to both yourself and the experience. Being entirely present opens the door to endless possibilities.

Being entirely present while practicing the exercises means "being in your body" and aware of what you feel while making a swing and hitting the golf ball. Ultimately it means allowing your body to talk to you by observing the following:

- The weight of the clubhead and its momentum as you swing.

- The feel of impact in your hands. (If you hit the ball on the sweet spot of the clubface, it should feel like "nothing," as opposed to a "shock.")

- Whether or not the rotation of your body feels effortless.

- If your arms feel like they're *trying* to swing the golf club or simply *allowing* gravity to carry out the energy of the rotation of your body to the golf club.

- The natural release of the clubhead through the ball as your hands, wrists, and arms rotate naturally and effortlessly to square the clubface.

- The difference between conscious control and effortless freedom, or flow.

Practice with a Partner

Since you may more readily recognize your own instinctive genius while witnessing it in another person, the exercises are often best explored with a partner. This way each player can share and receive feedback regarding whatever was felt, sensed, or learned. Such exchanges, unlike the more customary commiserations between golfers, involve collaboration.

The ideal question after a partner's success with an exercise might be, "What did you feel?" Encourage them to explore their potential. When you consciously or unconsciously attempt instead to limit someone, you are actually limiting yourself. When you encourage someone, you're likely to receive the same consideration in return. Encouragement is contagious!

You can't hold a man down without staying down with him.

—Booker T. Washington

Ultimately, when you go to the golf course to play golf, you can recapture your personal rhythm and flow by simply returning to your awareness of the feelings in your body. Don't try to figure out your personal rhythm and flow, because you can't! Just *be in your body*, connect with your internal senses, and play golf!

Chapter 7

Forty Instinct-Awakening Golf Exercises

The instinct-awakening golf exercises in this chapter will help you find your flow. When performing them, keep the following points in mind:

- Start with chip/pitch shots and half-swing full shots of fifty to one hundred yards with a pitching wedge in order to build feel.

- Simulate the movement of each exercise with a few initial practice swings to facilitate feel.

- Don't try to accomplish anything other than solid impact and trust the brilliance of your body/mind's kinesthetic intelligence.

- On the lines following each exercise, record your experience of it, including the results and what you felt or sensed in your body. Your comments will be invaluable for recognizing your adaptive instincts and tracking your progress as time passes.

The purpose of these exercises is to awaken your instinctive kinesthetic intelligence. For easy reference, each exercise is categorized by the aspect of the body or swing involved in stimulating that awareness: eyes, subtle senses, pre-shot activity, grip, and swing.

1. Eyes Follow Ball

(Eyes)

Allow your eyes to follow
the ball off the clubface
as soon as possible after impact.

Chip/Pitch: OK __ Good __ Very good __

Full Shots: OK __ Good __ Very good __

Comments:_____

_____

_____

_____

_____

_____

_____

2. Center of Chest

(Subtle senses)

Make the only focus for your swing be to feel
the center of your chest making your swing
and allow your arms, hands, and golf club
to respond to the movement.

Chip/Pitch: OK __ Good __ Very good __

Full Shots: OK __ Good __ Very good __

Comments:_____

_____

_____

_____

_____

_____

3. Figure Eight Movement
(Pre-shot activity)

a. Standing up straight without a golf club,
similar to a figure eight movement
continuously alternate moving your right hip bone
in a horizontal clockwise movement
and your left hip bone in a
horizontal counterclockwise movement.
Repeat for as long as feels comfortable.

b. Hit the ball with a similar feel,
allowing your body to just respond to the movement.

Chip/Pitch: OK ___ Good ___ Very good ___

Full Shots: OK ___ Good ___ Very good ___

Comments:_____

_____

_____

_____

_____

_____

_____

4. Scissor Grip

(Grip)

Using a ten-finger, overlap, or interlock grip,
place your right index finger across the top of the grip
so that the grip is "scissored" between
your right middle and index fingers, and:

a. Have your right thumb off the grip

b. Have your right thumb on the grip

c. Have your right thumb resting on
the outside of your right index finger

In each instance, allow the weight of the clubhead to swing.

Chip/Pitch	Full Shots
a. OK __ Good __ Very good __	OK __ Good __ Very good __
b. OK __ Good __ Very good __	OK __ Good __ Very good __
c. OK __ Good __ Very good __	OK __ Good __ Very good __

Comments:_____

_____

_____

_____

_____

_____

5. Crossover

(Swing)

Address the golf ball with a closed stance
with your right toes even with your left heel,
the ball position just inside your left foot,
and your hands even with your left thigh.

As you hit the ball, allow your right leg
to step over the ball position, with your torso following,
so that your right foot is on the right side of the target line
and your right toes are facing the target at
the finish of your swing.

Chip/Pitch: OK __ Good __ Very good __

Full Shots: OK __ Good __ Very good __

Comments:_____

_____

_____

_____

_____

_____

6. Eyes across Target Line

(Eyes)

Make the only focus for your swing be—
as soon as possible after impact—
to look up at a person who would be standing
face-on directly across the target line.

Chip/Pitch: OK __ Good __ Very good __

Full Shots: OK __ Good __ Very good __

Comments:_____

_____

_____

_____

_____

_____

_____

7. Eyes Closed after Impact

(Eyes)

Make the only focus for your swing be to close your eyes
as your head comes up on your follow-through
and keep your eyes closed until you anticipate
the ball would be landing on the ground.

Chip/Pitch: OK ___ Good ___ Very good ___

Full Shots: OK ___ Good ___ Very good ___

Comments:_____

_____

_____

_____

_____

_____

_____

8. Splatter the Wall with Paint
(Pre-shot activity)

a. Standing up straight without a golf club,
facing an imaginary golf ball and target line
visualize a wall five to ten feet high to your right.

Visualize and make the motion of dipping an imaginary
paintbrush in paint with your right hand,
then in one continuous motion shake the paint off
the paintbrush so it splatters the wall from ceiling to floor.

Repeat dipping the imaginary paintbrush in paint and
making the splattering motion several times.

b. Hit the ball with a similar feel.

Chip/Pitch: OK __ Good __ Very good __
Full shots: OK __ Good __ Very good __

Comments:_____

_____

_____

_____

_____

_____

_____

9. Dandelion Stem

(Pre-shot activity)

a. Standing up straight with your left palm resting on the end of the golf club, with the clubhead on the ground opposite the toes of your left foot, visualize a very strong dandelion stem five to six feet tall to your right.

Visualize and make the motion of pulling the stem down with your right hand under your left arm with enough force to scatter the flower seeds at the top of the stem.

Repeat several times.

b. Hit the ball with a similar feel.

Chip/Pitch: OK __ Good __ Very good __

Full shots: OK __ Good __ Very good __

Comments:_____

_____

_____

_____

_____

_____

10. Right Knee Pump

(Swing)

Make the only focus for your swing be—
on your follow-through—
to release your right foot from the ground
and gently pump your right knee toward the target.

Chip/Pitch: OK __ Good __ Very good __

Full shots: OK __ Good __ Very good __

Comments:_____

_____

_____

_____

_____

_____

_____

11. Eyes Forward

(Eyes)

a. As soon as possible after impact
look at the target.

b. As soon as possible after impact
look at the horizon beyond the target.

Chip/Pitch	Full Shots
a. OK __ Good __ Very good __	OK __ Good __ Very good __
b. OK __ Good __ Very good __	OK __ Good __ Very good __

Comments:_____

_____

_____

_____

_____

_____

_____

12. Slap the Dummy

(Pre-shot activity)

a. Standing up straight without a golf club, visualize a soft and flexible life-size dummy secured to the ground by its feet, standing just to the left of, and behind, your left foot.

Make the rotational motion of slapping the dummy firmly in the chest with the back of your left hand, and repeat several times.

b. Hit the ball with a subtly similar feel.

c. Slap the dummy in the chest with the palm of your right hand several times.

d. Hit the ball with a subtly similar feel.

Chip/Pitch	Full Shots
b. OK __ Good __ Very good __	OK __ Good __ Very good __
d. OK __ Good __ Very good __	OK __ Good __ Very good __

Comments:_____

_____

_____

_____

_____

13. Active Rotation

(Pre-shot activity)

a. Standing up straight without a golf club,
for as many times as feels comfortable
alternate between turning to the right
and pointing your right index finger
toward the sky behind you, then turning to the left and
pointing your left index finger toward the sky behind you.
Allow your body to respond to the movement.

b. Hit the ball with a subtly similar feel.

Chip/Pitch: OK __ Good __ Very good __

Full shots: OK __ Good __ Very good __

Comments:_____

_____

_____

_____

_____

_____

14. Pinky Fingernails

(Grip)

a. With a ten-finger grip, have the fingernail of your right pinky finger resting against the right side of the grip.

b. With your normal grip, have the fingernail of your left pinky finger resting against the left side of the grip.

c. With a ten-finger grip, have both pinky fingernails resting against the sides of the grip.

Chip/Pitch	Full Shots
a. OK __ Good __ Very good __	OK __ Good __ Very good __
b. OK __ Good __ Very good __	OK __ Good __ Very good __
c. OK __ Good __ Very good __	OK __ Good __ Very good __

Comments:_____

_____

_____

_____

_____

_____

_____

15. Step Forward & Step Back

(Swing)

a. After impact, take a small step forward,
first with your right foot and then with your left
so that your feet, toes, and the front of your body
are facing the target, with the shaft of the golf club
in a vertical position in front of your chest.

b. After impact, take several small steps back from the target,
with your feet, toes, and the front of your body
facing the target,
with the shaft of the golf club in a vertical position
in front of your chest.

Chip/Pitch	Full Shots
a. OK __ Good __ Very good __	OK __ Good __ Very good __
b. OK __ Good __ Very good __	OK __ Good __ Very good __

Comments:_____

_____

_____

_____

_____

_____

_____

16. Split & Scissor

(Grip)

Allow the weight of the clubhead
to swing for each of the following movements:

a. With a slightly split grip,
wrap your left thumb around the right side of the grip
and your right thumb around the left side of the grip
and "scissor" the grip between your
right middle and index fingers.

b. Using your normal grip, hit the ball
with a similar feel.

	Chip/Pitch	Full Shots
a.	OK __ Good __ Very good __	OK __ Good __ Very good __
b.	OK __ Good __ Very good __	OK __ Good __ Very good __

Comments:_____

_____

_____

_____

_____

17. Eyes High

(Eyes)

Before taking your address,
visualize the golf ball at its highest trajectory
for the shot you want to hit.

At address before starting your swing,
visualize that highest trajectory.

Make the only focus for your swing be to allow
your eyes to see the golf ball at that highest point
on your follow-through.

Chip/Pitch: OK __ Good __ Very good __

Full shots: OK __ Good __ Very good __

Comments:_____

_____

_____

_____

_____

_____

_____

18. Wrist Hinge

(Grip)

Grip the golf club at the bottom of the grip
with your right thumb and index finger on the shaft.

a. Hit the ball by making your swing
with only your hands and a wrist hinge.

b. Same as (a) and add some shoulder turn.

Chip/Pitch	Full Shots
a. OK __ Good __ Very good __	OK __ Good __ Very good __
b. OK __ Good __ Very good __	OK __ Good __ Very good __

Comments:_____

_____

_____

_____

_____

_____

19. Toss the Trash

(Pre-shot activity)

a. Visualize and make the movement of carrying a bag of garbage in your right hand behind your right buttock.

Walk toward an imaginary dumpster and make the movement of tossing the bag into the dumpster with a whirling sidearm motion.

Walk in a circle and repeat the motion several times.

b. Hit the ball with a similar feel.

Chip/Pitch: OK __ Good __ Very good __

Full shots: OK __ Good __ Very good __

Comments:_____

_____

_____

_____

_____

_____

_____

20. Start the Mower

(Pre-shot activity)

a. Standing up straight without a golf club,
visualize a lawn mower
with a pull-cord engine opposite your left foot.

With the pull-cord handle extended
in front of your right hip,
gently but firmly pull the cord with your right hand
above your right shoulder to "start the engine."
Repeat several times.

b. Hit the ball with a similar feel.

Chip/Pitch: OK __ Good __ Very good __

Full shots: OK __ Good __ Very good __

Comments:_____

_____

_____

_____

_____

_____

_____

21. The Snake

(Subtle senses)

Make the only focus for your swing be:

a. To visualize and make your golf swing feel like your body is a long, strong slithering snake.

b. Same as (a) and imitate the motion of the snake, such as a cobra, biting and recoiling at impact.

Chip/Pitch	Full Shots
a. OK __ Good __ Very good __	OK __ Good __ Very good __
b. OK __ Good __ Very good __	OK __ Good __ Very good __

Comments:_____

_____

_____

_____

_____

_____

_____

22. The Soft Snake
(Subtle senses)

Make your only focus be to feel like you are making your swing from below your knees.

Chip Shots: OK __ Good __ Very good __

Pitch Shots: OK __ Good __ Very good __

Full Shots: OK __ Good __ Very good __

Comments:_____

_____

_____

_____

_____

_____

_____

23. Feel Lag

(Subtle senses)

Make the only focus for your swing be
to sense the golf club "lag" your left elbow
by feeling your left elbow lead the golf club
on your forward swing.

Chip/Pitch: OK __ Good __ Very good __

Full shots: OK __ Good __ Very good __

Comments:_____

_____

_____

_____

_____

_____

_____

24. Throw Right Palm

(Subtle senses)

Make the only focus for your swing be
to feel like you are "throwing"
the palm of your right hand at the golf ball
on your forward swing through impact.

Chip/Pitch: OK __ Good __ Very good __

Full shots: OK __ Good __ Very good __

Comments:_____

_____

_____

_____

_____

_____

_____

25. Split Grip & Brush the Grass
(Pre-shot activity)

a. With a split grip and the clubhead about
six to eight inches above the ground at address,
make half swings and brush the grass
on your forward swing.
Repeat as many times as feels comfortable.

b. Using your normal grip and address,
hit the ball with a similar feel.

Chip/Pitch: OK __ Good __ Very good __

Full shots: OK __ Good __ Very good __

Comments:_____

_____

_____

_____

_____

_____

_____

26. Tennis Overspin

(Pre-shot activity)

a. Standing up straight without a golf club,
visualize and make the motion of
swinging a tennis racket with your right hand
from low to high, putting tremendous overspin
on an imaginary tennis ball.

b. Hit the golf ball with a similar feel.

Chip/Pitch: OK __ Good __ Very good __

Full shots: OK __ Good __ Very good __

Comments:_____

_____

_____

_____

_____

_____

_____

27. Right Thumb Rotation

(Subtle senses)

Make the only focus for your swing
be to feel the tip of your right thumb
rotating through impact
to point toward the target.

Chip/Pitch: OK __ Good __ Very good __

Full shots: OK __ Good __ Very good __

Comments:_____

_____

_____

_____

_____

_____

_____

28. Counting Hang Time

(Subtle senses)

Make the only focus for your swing
be to count the number of seconds
the golf ball is in the air.

Chip/Pitch: OK __ Good __ Very good __

Full shots: OK __ Good __ Very good __

Comments:_____

_____

_____

_____

_____

_____

_____

29. Field Goal

(Subtle senses)

Visualize hitting a shot over the crossbar and
between the uprights of a football goal post.
As soon as possible after impact,
drop the golf club to the ground and raise both arms
to make the referee's successful field goal signal.

Chip/Pitch: OK __ Good __ Very good __

Full shots: OK __ Good __ Very good __

Comments:_____

_____

_____

_____

_____

_____

_____

30. Eyes in Back of Head

(Subtle senses)

Make the only focus for your swing be to imagine
that you have eyes in back of your head
and, after impact, use them to imagine looking down
the target line away from the target.

Chip/Pitch: OK __ Good __ Very good __

Full shots: OK __ Good __ Very good __

Comments:_____

_____

_____

_____

_____

_____

_____

31. Low Draw/Slice Fix

(Subtle senses)

For a low shot or a draw,
make the only focus for your swing
be to feel like you are:

a. "Polishing" the outside of the golf ball with
the palm of your right hand through impact.

b. "Polishing" the outside of the golf ball with
the clubface through impact.

Chip/Pitch	Full Shots
a. OK __ Good __ Very good __	OK __ Good __ Very good __
b. OK __ Good __ Very good __	OK __ Good __ Very good __

Comments:_____

_____

_____

_____

_____

_____

_____

32. Point Index Finger

(Swing)

a. As soon as possible after impact,
release your right hand from the grip
and point your right index finger
to where you want the ball to land.

b. With a ten-finger grip,
as soon as possible after impact
release your left hand from the grip
and point your left index finger
to where you want the ball to land.

Chip/Pitch	Full Shots
a. OK __ Good __ Very good __	OK __ Good __ Very good __
b. OK __ Good __ Very good __	OK __ Good __ Very good __

Comments:_____

_____

_____

_____

_____

_____

33. Peripheral Vision

(Eyes)

a. While focusing your eyes on the ground
five to ten feet forward of the golf ball,
make several practice swings, brushing the grass.

b. Hit the golf ball with
a soft focus of your eyes on the ground
one to two feet forward of the golf ball
while "seeing" the ball in your peripheral vision.

Chip/Pitch: OK __ Good __ Very good __

Full shots: OK __ Good __ Very good __

Comments:_____

_____

_____

_____

_____

_____

_____

34. Hand & Palm Rotation

(Subtle senses)

a. Make the only focus for your swing be
to feel the back of your left hand
turn toward the ground after impact.

b. Make the only focus for your swing be
to feel the palm of your right hand
turn toward the ground after impact.

Chip/Pitch	Full Shots
a. OK __ Good __ Very good __	OK __ Good __ Very good __
b. OK __ Good __ Very good __	OK __ Good __ Very good __

Comments:_____

_____

_____

_____

_____

_____

_____

35. Release the Water

(Subtle senses)

Imagine the shaft of the golf club is
one-quarter filled with water
and there is a hole at the bottom of the shaft
with a very soft membrane holding the water in.

Make the only focus for your forward swing be
to feel like you are "releasing" the water
through the membrane
toward a spot on the ground
just forward of the golf ball.

Chip/Pitch: OK __ Good __ Very good __

Full shots: OK __ Good __ Very good __

Comments:_____

_____

_____

_____

_____

_____

_____

36. Grip Variations

(Grip)

a. Extend your left index finger down the left side of the grip with the tip curled on the underneath side of the grip and resting on the web between your right ring and middle fingers.

The tops of your right pinky and ring fingers will be resting on the inside of your left index finger with your left thumb fitting perfectly in the palm of your right hand.

b. Same as (a) and "scissor" the grip between your right middle and index fingers, with your right thumb on the grip.

c. Same as (b) but have your right thumb resting on the outside of your right index finger.

d. Using your normal grip, hit the ball with a similar feel.

Chip/Pitch	½ PW Full Shots
a. OK __ Good __ Very good __	OK __ Good __ Very good __
b. OK __ Good __ Very good __	OK __ Good __ Very good __
c. OK __ Good __ Very good __	OK __ Good __ Very good __
d. OK __ Good __ Very good __	OK __ Good __ Very good __

Comments:_____

_____

_____

_____

_____

37. Follow-Through Variations
(Swing)

a. Finish your follow-through with your hands close to your left ribs and the shaft of the golf club in a vertical position.

b. At the finish of your follow-through, "recoil" the golf club and put the grip end of the club in an imaginary "holster" on your left hip.

Chip/Pitch	Full Shots
a. OK __ Good __ Very good __	OK __ Good __ Very good __
b. OK __ Good __ Very good __	OK __ Good __ Very good __

Comments:_____

_____

_____

_____

_____

_____

_____

38. Left Hand Low Shuffle

(Pre-shot activity)

a. Hold a 9 iron or a PW with a slightly split left hand low grip, with both thumbs wrapped around the sides of the grip.

Start with your feet together and, with your body facing the target line, take small "shuffle" steps toward the target while making continuous small swings back and forth, brushing the grass along the target line. Repeat several times.

b. With your normal grip and stance, hit the ball with a similar feel in your hands.

Chip/Pitch: OK __ Good __ Very good __

Full shots: OK __ Good __ Very good __

Comments:_____

_____

_____

_____

_____

_____

_____

39. Curl, Shuffle & Brush

(Pre-shot activity)

a. Hold a 9 iron or a PW with a slightly split grip, with both thumbs wrapped around the sides of the grip. Have both index fingers extended down the sides of the grip and curled on the underneath side of the grip.

Start with your feet together and,
with your body facing the target line,
take small "shuffle" steps toward the target while
making continuous small swings back and forth,
brushing the grass along the target line.
Repeat several times.

b. With your normal grip and stance,
hit the ball with a similar feel in your hands.

Chip/Pitch: OK __ Good __ Very good __

Full shots: OK __ Good __ Very good __

Comments:_____

_____

_____

_____

_____

_____

_____

40. Left-Handed Tennis Backhand
(Pre-shot activity)

a. Standing up straight without a golf club,
visualize and make the motion of
holding a tennis racket in your left hand
as would a left-handed tennis player.

Make the rotational movement of
hitting a two-handed backhand shot.
Repeat several times.

b. Hit the ball with a similar feel.

Chip/Pitch: OK __ Good __ Very good __
Full shots: OK __ Good __ Very good __

Comments:_____

_____

_____

_____

_____

_____

_____

Conclusion

By regularly exploring the exercises in this book, you will continue to discover that your subconscious body/mind is more than capable—it is genius. May you learn to trust it and let go of your conscious mind's interference in your golf game. And may your inner golfer, once awakened, soon have you mastering the game.

If this approach to learning has helped you with your golf game, what other "conventional wisdom" or "standard procedures" might you start questioning in your life?

Do you *see* only what you were taught to see?
Do you *hear* only what you were taught to hear?
Are you *aware* only of what you were taught to think?

Deep inside…you know.
And if you go a little deeper…
you know that you know!

With even deeper insight and awareness
you may find the
"I Can," "I Know," and maybe even the
"I AM"!

Notes

CHAPTER 3

1. Susan L. Smalley, PhD, and Diana Winston, *Fully Present: The Science, Art, and Practice of Mindfulness* (Boston: Da Capo Press, 2010), 11.

2. Ibid., 61.

CHAPTER 4

1. Dr. Joseph Parent, *Zen Golf: Mastering the Mental Game* (New York: Doubleday, 2002), 38.

CHAPTER 5

1. Chuck Hogan, *Rethinking Golf: A New Approach to Performance in the 21st Century* (Bend, OR: Maverick Publications), 72.

2. Parent, *Zen Golf*, 63.

About the Author

Jerry Brown grew up hitting golf balls on a narrow strip of land in his grandmother's yard on Long Island, New York, with trees on one side and a road on the other. By age ten he had learned how to hit a ball straight and solidly through feel rather than strength.

An all-around athlete, at age twelve he broke a leg while skiing and soon after was diagnosed with other serious health issues that led to lasting physical ill-effects. Though many people would have given up hope for an active life, he persevered.

Brown graduated from Rollins College in Winter Park, Florida, with a BA in business and economics. Qualifying for the school golf team as a senior, he played among a group of highly ranked Division II athletes, including a future PGA Tour winner. Subsequently working as an independent insurance agent for thirty years, he played competitive golf in the New York metropolitan area until the late 1980s, while facing yet other serious medical challenges.

Over a period of many years, he refined a series of exercises to maintain his golf game. In 2012, he moved to Santa Fe, New Mexico, where he combined his practice of golf with a growing interest in Eastern philosophy and spiritual lessons, incorporating an "inner" approach to developing a pure golf swing. His love of coaching led him to produce this book, which he hopes will improve golfers' games and inspire them in all walks of life.

Today, still learning about the body/mind relationship in health as well as golf, Brown is pleased to be called "a lifetime learner," believing that when we stop learning we stop living.

For more information and to purchase
additional copies of this book,
please visit his website:
www.keepitsimplegolf.com.